E
177.1
Amo.

D1237920

# Being Helpful

By Janine Amos  Illustrated by Annabel Spenceley
Consultant Rachael Underwood

**Gareth Stevens Publishing**
A WORLD ALMANAC EDUCATION GROUP COMPANY

Please visit our web site at: www.garethstevens.com
For a free color catalog describing Gareth Stevens Publishing's
list of high-quality books and multimedia programs,
call 1-800-542-2595 (USA) or 1-800-387-3178 (Canada).
Gareth Stevens Publishing's fax: (414) 332-3567.

Library of Congress Cataloging-in-Publication Data

Amos, Janine.
      Being helpful / by Janine Amos; illustrated by Annabel Spenceley.
        p. cm. — (Courteous kids)
      Includes bibliographical references.
      Summary: Provides examples and tips for being helpful when one
is with others.
      ISBN 0-8368-3169-1 (lib. bdg.)
      1. Cooperativeness—Juvenile literature. [1. Cooperativeness.
2. Helpfulness. 3. Conduct of life.] I. Spenceley, Annabel, ill. II. Title.
BJ1533.C74A65   2002
177'.7—dc21                  2002018764

This edition first published in 2002 by
**Gareth Stevens Publishing**
A World Almanac Education Group Company
330 West Olive Street, Suite 100
Milwaukee, Wisconsin 53212 USA

Gareth Stevens editor: JoAnn Early Macken
Cover Design: Katherine A. Goedheer

This edition © 2002 by Gareth Stevens, Inc. First published by Cherrytree Press,
a subsidiary of Evans Brothers Limited. © 1997 by Cherrytree (a member of the
Evans Group of Publishers), 2A Portman Mansions, Chiltern Street, London
W1M 1LE, United Kingdom. This U.S. edition published under license from
Evans Brothers Limited. Additional end matter © 2002 by Gareth Stevens, Inc.

All rights reserved. No part of this book may be reproduced, stored in a
retrieval system, or transmitted in any form or by any means, electronic,
mechanical, photocopying, recording, or otherwise, without the prior
written permission of the copyright holder.

Printed in the United States of America

1 2 3 4 5 6 7 8 9 06 05 04 03 02

# Note to Parents and Teachers

The questions that appear in **boldface** type can be used to initiate
discussion with your children or class. Encourage them to think of
possible answers before continuing with the story.

# Li and Joseph

21. ԲՐ ALP (02) 30p. (02)

It's cleanup time.

"Let's put everything away," says Dave,
"so we'll be able to find it tomorrow."

5

Joseph puts the blocks back in their box.

Li puts the dough back in its tub.

Li finds a block in the dough,
so he takes it to Joseph.

Joseph is finished putting away
all of the blocks.

Li is still busy.
**What could Joseph do?**

Joseph goes over to Li.
"I can help you," he says.
**How does Li feel?**

Joseph and Li put away the rest
of the dough together.

"We're done!" says Joseph.

"You worked together," says Dave.
"You helped each other."

# Harry and Rosie

Rosie is crying.

"She's been crying all morning!"
Mom says to Harry.

"Do you want your rattle, Rosie?" asks Mom.

City Carnegie Library
West Broadway

"No!" says Rosie.

19

"Do you want your bottle, Rosie?" asks Mom.

"No!" says Rosie.

The telephone rings. Rosie cries harder.
"Oh, no!" says Mom.

How does Mom feel?
What could Harry do?

Harry goes over to Rosie.

He makes a funny face.

Rosie smiles.

Harry wiggles his fingers.

Rosie laughs.

Harry laughs, too.
"She's happy now," says Harry.

29

"Thanks, Harry," says Mom.

"You helped Rosie, and that helped me."

Sometimes, people need help.
Maybe you know something you can do
to make another person's problem better, or
you can ask the other person how you can help.
You might need help yourself if you have
a problem. Who could you ask to help you?

## More Books to Read

*Rotten Ralph Helps Out.* Jack Gantos
(Farrar, Strauss, and Giroux)

*Sing, Sophie!* Dayle Ann Dodds (Candlewick Press)

*Somewhere Today: A Book of Peace.*
Shelley Moore Thomas (Albert Whitman)